'Get a Life'

And other sketches for your youth group

'Get a Life'

And other sketches for your youth group

Tony Bower, Edmund Farrow, Matt Sands

Scripture Union

Scripture Union, 207–209 Queensway, Bletchley, Milton Keynes, MK2 2EB, England.

© Edmund Farrow, Matt Sands, Tony Bower 1998

First published 1998

ISBN 1-85999-232-3
All rights reserved. Permission is given to photocopy the sketches in *Get a Life*. Other than these, no part of this publication may be reproduced, stored in a retrieval system, or transmitted, in any form or by any means, electronic, mechanical, photocopying, recording or otherwise, without the prior permission of Scripture Union. These sketches may not be performed for a paying audience without the prior permission of Scripture Union.
The right of Edmund Farrow, Matt Sands and Tony Bower to be identified as authors of this work has been asserted by them in accordance with the Copyright, Designs and Patents Act 1988.

British Library Cataloguing-in-Publication Data

A catalogue record for this book is available from the British Library.

Cover design and illustration by Blue Pig Design Co.

Printed and bound in Great Britain by Ebenezer Baylis & Son Limited, The Trinity Press, Worcester and London.

CONTENTS

INTRODUCTION

I recently visited a youth meeting. When the 'talkie bit' was about to begin, the group were led into the 'room'. When they spotted the TV and video set up, there was a virtually unanimous groan: 'Oh no! Not *another* video!' OK, so I've exaggerated it a little, but it just shows how easy it is for all of us to get stuck in a rut, trying to communicate in the same way, week in, week out.

Get a Life is here to help us as we communicate the good news in our youth programmes. Drama is a wonderful tool that we don't use enough. Whether the sketches have been thoroughly rehearsed and every line learnt by two understudies, or whether the 'actors' have picked up the photocopied scripts five minutes beforehand, drama is truly interactive, with the wonderful element of audience participation that only a live sketch can provide. This can have the great advantage of breaking down barriers in order for there to be a free and serious discussion later in the evening. It also allows us to involve the young people in the production themselves, so that it becomes their meeting or event rather than ours.

All the sketches in *Get a Life* have been chosen for their youth-friendly approach. They come in a variety of styles. Some need more time and preparation than others, but there are handy tips on props, costumes and staging before each sketch.

The sketches in *Get a Life* approach themes and issues that are relevant to young people. Each one is followed by a series of questions, or discussion starters. These questions don't come with any set answers but they are designed to get your group thinking. Each sketch also has a list of Bible references after it. These references either contain a passage on the theme of the sketch or a passage that bears some relevance to the discussion starters. They are not intended to be exhaustive; they are simply a springboard for discussion. Feel free to tailor the passages and discussion starters to the needs of your own group.

Drama can be unpredictable, but hey, enjoy it! Making mistakes, getting lines wrong or missing cues, is part of being human. If your group see that you are a normal human being who makes mistakes, it's a lot easier for them to open up. However, it is always important to remain confident and keep the flow of the sketch going – even when you're going wrong. If all else fails, improvise!

Drama should be enjoyed and the majority of sketches here contain humour. Make sure they're enjoyed, however, not just by the audience, but by the performers themselves. After all, when we were called to spread the word, no one said we couldn't enjoy it!

GET A LIFE

Edmund Farrow

THEME: Who am I? / Self-worth / Peer pressure

HANDY TIPS:

Props: *a selection of open boxes labelled 'SALE', 'BARGAINS!', 'ARMY SURPLUS'; a table; a shop counter with pen and paper on it; a large unmarked box; a mobile phone; a university scarf; a brightly coloured shoebox; toy money (optional); a crash helmet; a first aid kit/box; a Pick'n'Mix bag containing one or two cuddly toys, a phone book and various hats, eg headscarf, baseball hat; a calculator; a credit card; a badge in the shape of a wooden cross; a skimpy dress.*

8–9 minutes

CHARACTERS:

Riler: the archetypal slimy salesman with an ingratiating smile, smarmy voice and enough gel in his hair to cause an environmental disaster if he ever went swimming in the sea. Even he, however, is forced to rethink his life as events unfold and his values and his wallet are threatened.

Gill: a cynical, trendy student who thinks her 'square' room-mate Jackie should get a life.

Jackie: unable to get a word in while Gill and Riler plan her life for her.

Barry: well, how can we describe Barry? A control freak? An adrenalin junkie? A man two tent pegs short of a wilderness survival kit? Probably all of these and more. He gives the impression of having received one too many rugby injuries to the head.

Darren: the man for whom the term 'anorak' was invented. He seems permanently phased out and talks in a regional accent. He has an air of apathy about him.

Sally: a shy, polite girl who desperately wants to be liked and loved.

Tracy: a self-conscious new Christian. She knows that she has done the right thing in being born again, but she lacks the experience and the knowledge to explain exactly how things have changed. All she is certain of is that things have changed and for the better.

The scene is set inside a shop. There is a selection of open boxes on a table at the back of the stage with signs on them saying 'SALE', 'ARMY SURPLUS' and 'BARGAINS!'. There is a counter of some sort stage right, with another box on it (containing Riler's selection of lifestyles) and a pen and paper. The box has a sign on it reading 'PLEASE PAY HERE'. A phone rings off-stage and Riler enters behind the counter, carrying his mobile phone.

Riler: Hello? Get-A-Life Incorporated – new and used lifestyles for the discerning shopper. How can I help you? ... A gift for your son? Yes, that can be arranged. Can you give me the details of your order? ... Gifted musician, yes... *(Riler writes the details down as he repeats them.)* Rugby scholarship, no problem... Well-paid medical consultant, yes... Right, yes, we can have that life off to you in a couple of days. Would you like it gift-wrapped? ... Of course, yes... *(Gill and Jackie enter the shop from stage left. Gill starts poking around in the boxes. Jackie looks as though she wants to be somewhere else.)* Yes... thank you... How much will that cost? Oh, you wouldn't believe how much ... How old did you say your son was again? ... Three months! Well, congratulations Mr Jackson... Yes, thank you, yes, I'll see to it immediately. Good-bye... *(He puts the phone away and starts to yell off-stage. Gill drags Jackie over to speak to him.)* Oy Rob! Dust off another Parental Expectation Special...

Gill: Excuse me, I was wondering if you can do anything for my room-mate here. She works far too hard. She's always studying – it's like she's actually interested in her subject. She gets up way too early and is just sickeningly nice. I think it's about time she got a life.

Jackie: Er, I'm not really sure...

Riler: Well you've certainly come to the right place. Here at Get-A-Life Incorporated, we have all sorts of lifestyles specially tailored to suit the individual. You won't find a wider selection of ways to live anywhere else, and I think I know just the thing you're looking for... *(He starts rummaging in his box.)*

Gill: Sounds great.

Jackie: Look, I really don't know if...

Riler: Here we are! *(He pulls out a brightly coloured box and shows the items inside to Gill.)* 'The Turn On, Tune In and Drop Out Starter Kit': a four-pack of lager, three orange tablets, two little plastic bags containing questionable substances, oh, and a ...... *(insert name of band)* CD. She'll be failing her degree within a semester.

Gill: How much is that?

Riler: Ninety-five pounds and two years suspended.

Jackie: Er...

Gill: Great! *(She hands him some money and takes the box.)* There you go. Bye. *(Gill and Jackie exit as Barry enters carrying a crash helmet.)*

Riler: Bye... Can I help you, sir?

Barry: Er, yes, I'd like you to look over this life I bought from you five years ago. *(He hands the helmet to Riler. Meanwhile,*

Darren enters and starts rummaging in the boxes.)

Riler: Ah, a Complete Nutter 2000. I haven't seen one of these in a long time. You just can't get the parts these days. *(He sucks in air through his teeth.)* I'm afraid this is going to be expensive. What's the problem exactly?

Barry: Well, it worked fine at first. I started with some fairly tame parachuting and mountain climbing, then moved on to snorkelling in shark-infested waters and then finally to blindfold paragliding. But I just can't seem to get the same buzz of danger from it any more. The thrill's gone out of my life.

Riler: Ah, a common problem with the 2000 model. I'm afraid you need to upgrade. I think what you need is the bungee kayaking attachment.

Barry: What?

(Riler pulls a first aid kit out of his box and walks round beside Barry.)

Riler: Combine the thrills of white water rafting with the bone-jarring insanity of bungee jumping by steering a canoe over a waterfall *(his voice builds to a crescendo)* and plummeting into the raging torrent!

Barry: *(uncertainly)* Er...

Riler: *(conversationally)* It's quite fun apparently, if a little damp.

Barry: How much?

Riler: *(matter-of-factly)* Fifty pounds a throw and six months in hospital.

Barry: What the heck - I'll try anything once. *(He hands over some money. Darren approaches the counter, carrying a Pick'n'Mix bag from one of the boxes at the back.)*

Riler: Thanks very much. *(Barry exits.)* What a nutter... Can I help you, sir?

Darren: I'd like to buy this, please.

Riler: Certainly. *(He puts the bag inside his own box and pretends to rummage through it.)* The Pick'n'Mix lifestyle is very popular these days. Let me see. Ah, you're obviously an expert on spiritual matters, sir. *(Riler briefly pulls some of the items – depending on what props are available – out of his box as he mentions them, eg cuddly toys for idols, a phone book for the mantras, etc.)* Some assorted idols, airfare to Mecca, book of mantras, assorted head gear of varying practicality, family pack of communion wafers... Hmm, I think that's about it... Oh, and an open mind.

Darren: I don't remember that.

Riler: That's 'cos it's so open there's nothing there any more.

Darren: Oh, right.

Riler: Don't worry, it's very fashionable. That'll be... *(Riler tots up some numbers on a calculator.)* Absolutely nothing at all – it's completely worthless. However, there's a handling fee of two hundred pounds and then the weekly spiritual counselling sessions exploring your inner self, at fourteen ninety-five an hour.

Darren: *(holding up a credit card)* Do you take plastic?

Riler: That will do nicely, sir. (*Sally enters as the transaction takes place and then steps forward uncertainly as Darren exits.*) There you go. Bye... Yes, miss?

Sally: I'd like a new lifestyle, please.

Riler: Which model are you interested in?

Sally: Well, I don't really know... I'd like people to take an interest in me. I want to make them laugh, I guess. I want to have lots of friends I can have a laugh with... Well... a boyfriend, actually... but the other friends sound good as well.

Riler: I think I have just the thing. 'The-Life-And-Soul-Of-The-Party' lifestyle. Here we go. (*He pulls out a skimpy dress from the box.*)

Sally: Well, er, I'm not sure...

Riler: You're guaranteed to have a man within a week. Says it right here.

Sally: Erm... What does it cost?

Riler: Your self-respect.

Sally: Erm... Done! (*She grabs the dress and leaves. Riler watches her go.*)

Riler: Bye... (*His smarmy grin fades.*) Bit of a shame, really. Seemed like a nice girl. I wonder if she would have been interested... I need to get a grip – I'll be believing my own patter next. No, business is business. (*Tracy enters and approaches the counter while Riler is still talking to himself. She is wearing a wooden cross as a badge.*) I've still got fifteen instalments due on the Merc.

Tracy: Excuse me, I'd like to return this life I bought from you last year. (*She holds out a university scarf.*)

Riler: Sorry, we don't do refunds. I can do you a straight swap though. What's wrong with it?

Tracy: Oh, there's nothing that much wrong with it, as such. I quite enjoyed it really. I just found a better one, that's all.

Riler: A better one? That's a fine quality life and my prices are the best in town.

Tracy: Well, yes, it is a nice life. It's just... well, there's a guy round the corner handing out better ones for free.

Riler: Free!

Tracy: Yes, to anyone who'll take them.

Riler: (*panicking*) I'm ruined! Let me have a look at it... (*She hands over the badge. Riler examines it closely.*) It's a bit rough – shoddy workmanship.

Tracy: I think it's meant to be like that. (*She takes it back.*)

Riler: Are you sure?

Tracy: It's ethnic.

Riler: (*sceptical*) Hmm! Is that what he said?

Tracy: Erm, I don't know. Look, I didn't understand everything he said, but he gave me his personal guarantee and there's on-site service for life.

Riler: Life!

Tracy: Er, quite a lot longer than that,

actually. Look it's got all these optional extras: love, joy, peace, patience, kindness...

Riler: Ah, that will be where the costs will start mounting up.

Tracy: Maybe... I don't know, but he seemed to be offering something different. I'm looking forward to spending some time with him and finding out some more. *(She becomes very self-conscious and hurries to leave.)* I think... I think I'm different as well. Look, I'm sorry. Here's your life back *(Tracy puts the scarf on the counter)*, you can keep it. I have to go. Goodbye. *(She smiles and exits.)*

Riler: Odd... *(He turns the scarf over in his hands.)* Hey, this is a deluxe model. He's giving out better than this for free? *(He yells off-stage and grabs his coat from under the counter.)* Er, Rob! Look after the shop. I'm just going out to... for a quick coffee... OK? *(Riler opens the door and hurries out. He calls after Tracy.)* Hey! Wait for me!

---

 1   What should be the differences between a Christian's life and a non-Christian's?

2   From your experience, what are the differences in reality?

3   Some people who aren't Christians have many fantastic qualities and are kind, compassionate and caring. So what's the difference between them and a Christian?

 John 10:10 (Living life to the full)

Luke 9:23–25 (Losing your life and saving it)

1 John 3:13 (Our identity now and our future hope of life)

Galatians 5:16–26 (Live by the Spirit)

SELF-HELP

Matt Sands

THEME: Self-image / Looking for fulfilment

HANDY TIPS:

Props: *table; tape player; tape.*

 7–8 minutes

CHARACTERS:

The man: a bit of a loser, preferably tall and skinny. Very gullible. Whoever plays him needs to really ham it up, so that he's almost like Mr Bean.

The voice: a real game show host voice: cheesy, tacky and American. It can be recorded onto a good quality tape, or can be spoken live off-stage through a microphone. To the audience, it should seem TOO unbelievable.

The sketch is a mime, with a pre-recorded voice giving our hero advice on becoming a better man. This is a one-man show, but the voice on the tape is equally vital to the sketch. The audience are just flies on the wall, watching the personal strivings of a man desperate to find his way.

The scene is a room, with a table. On the table is a tape player, facing the audience, or even better linked to the PA system. The man puts a tape into the player and presses play. He stretches his arms and smiles. The voice begins to speak.

Hullo... and thank *you* for buying this Oscar Weinstein self-help tape on 'How to be a New Man'. Please follow the instructions on this cassette and together we'll take you into new dimensions of manhood that you've never dreamed of. *(The man grins to the crowd, and looks pleased.)*

Are you tired of being Mr Nobody? *(He nods.)* Sick of having sand kicked in your face at the beach? *(Nods.)* Fed up with your zero personality? *(He looks confused but nods.)* Do you want to be a man people look at and say 'That's my kinda guy'? *(He nods vigorously.)* Well, it begins now – our journey together, as you discover 'the NEW man'. *(Our man gnashes his teeth and growls, flexing his arms.)*

Before we start, I want you to take a good look at yourself. Man, what a pathetic specimen you really are! *(The man looks at the tape player, both surprised and offended.)* Call those muscles? *(He flexes his biceps.)* I've seen sparrows with bigger kneecaps, and as for that stomach, well – you've got a belly spelt B-E-E-R, haven't you? *(He looks at his belly and is sad.)* Why you're not much of a man at all, are you? *(He is offended and goes to switch off the tape.)* Ah-hah-hah – don't switch me off! *(The man gazes at the tape player, very confused.)* These are things you need to hear, so you know where you are coming from. No more the puny, deluded weakling. Next stop the Olympian ideal! *(The man has got his faith back, and attempts to look noble and Olympian.)*

OK – your change into a new man will involve you changing in three areas: your mind, your body and your heart. Change in these three areas and my... even your dog won't recognise you! Now, in order to receive the full benefit of this tape, I want you to take off your shoes. *(The man looks confused.)* NOW please, we haven't got all day. *(He shrugs and pulls off shoes.)* And your socks. *(He removes his socks.)* Man, those feet sure smell *bad* don't they? Now, take a deep breath and you're ready to begin.

OK, part one: changing the mind. What's kicking around up there in that mind of yours? Worried? *(The man nods.)* Confused? *(He nods and his bottom lip wobbles.)* Can't sleep at night? What we need is a good old clear-out up there, isn't that right? Well, don't worry – that's easy. Just follow my instructions and you'll be taking the first step towards being a new man. OK now, just sit down cross-legged on the floor. *(The man obeys.)* That's it. Comfy? Good. Now, place your elbows on your knees and hands in the air. *(The man is in hippie meditation position.)* Good. OK, now close those eyes and begin to think... *(the voice gets all slow and dreamy)* peaceful thoughts... pure dazzling white, hosts of golden dandelions, the shimmering of a crystal dewdrop in the rays of the morning sun, reflecting a rainbow of pure colour into your senses. *(Throughout this, our man is getting all relaxed and is smiling, even puckering his lips as if kissing the air. He is far away.)* Clear away that junk – think only of these lovely things. And now repeat after me *(sounding very 'eastern' and droning)* Hmmmmmmmmm... *(The man repeats the long hum.)* That's good, and again... Hmmmmmmmmm... *(The man repeats it again.)* Good... last time. *(The voice does a really long hum which the man duly copies. He is now looking truly 'high'.)* Is that mind clearing up? *(The man nods.)* Good. OK, stand on your feet, but keep that mind clear and focused. You have a new brain now. *(The man smiles and claps his hands together.)*

OK, now you're ready to work on that body. In order to become a new man we must change that shapeless, skinny wreck into a bronzed, bulging temple of iron. *(The man pulls a pathetic bodybuilder pose.)* This will be done by enforcing a strict and brutal exercise regime. *(He looks nervous.)* OK, let's put you through your paces: the press-up position, please. *(The man unhappily adopts the press-up position.)* OK, are we ready? Here we go... *(The voice slows down.)* One *(the man shakily does a press-up)*, pause... and there you have it. *(The man beams and gets up.)* That wasn't too hard, was it? Keep going like that and you'll soon be Mr Universe instead of Mr I'm a Sad Pathetic Weed. OK. Feeling strong now are we? *(He nods and poses.)* Well it's important that with your new strength you become an agile athlete, so sit down on the floor please, with legs stretched out in front of you. *(He sits.)* OK, now reach out and take hold of your right foot. *(The man reaches and grabs his LEFT foot.)* No. I said your RIGHT foot. *(The man stares strangely at the player, and grabs right foot.)* That's better. Now, gently place it behind your head. *(The man man tries to, but his legs are long and gangly and he gets his leg about a foot off the floor, trying to bend under it. He looks stupid.)* There, doesn't that feel great... all those sinews and muscles in perfect harmony. *(He keeps trying.)* If you feel confident, why not try it with both feet. *(There is a pause while the man keeps trying. He rolls pathetically around on the floor and then gives up.)* Now, your body is transformed. No more weedy boy. Now you've the body of a real man.

Our final change is in your heart. It's no good having a new mind and body when your feelings and emotions are the old you, now is it? *(The man shakes his head.)* No, that's right. We at Oscar Weinstein have developed a new technique to make your heart feel as soft and tender as a baby's bottom. *(Pause, while the man touches his bottom.)* OK, part three: the heart.

Remember the movie *Home Alone*? *(He nods.)* Remember the old man who hasn't spoken to his son in years, and the only way he can see his lovely little granddaughter is to watch her sing Christmas carols in the church? *(The man nods and looks a little sad.)* Imagine you are Kevin on Christmas Day. *(At this point the voice begins to cry a little as he speaks, getting more maudlin as he goes on.)* You're looking through your window and the snow is falling gently outside. Your family are at home with you, and outside the kind old gentleman's son looks nervously at his dad. And then they embrace, and floods of tears pour down the old man's cheeks. *(By now the voice and our man are howling with tears. It's really over the top.)* The old man sees you in the window and raises a tiny hand to wave. It's so sad... they're reunited, on Christmas Day. *(Uncontrollable sobs.)* It's so sad. You feel all gooey inside. *(The man falls to his knees and wails.)* It's enough to make any real man cry. *(The voice slowly recovers composure.)* OK, now your heart is soft and ready to be in your new body. Let's give it a quick exercise before your transformation is complete. *(The man is standing now, ready.)* OK, deep breath. IN! *(The man sucks in air.)*... hold... and OUT! *(He exhales again.)* Again, deep breath... hold... and out! One more time... deep breath... hold... *(pause)*... and keep holding while I tell you about our latest self-help tape from Oscar Weinstein. *(As the voice drones on, the man is obviously struggling, and begins to turn purple.)* Tired of doing the weeding? Sick to death of your green beans? Then you need our latest tape, 'How to overcome being an obsessive gardener'. Let Oscar take away your passion for the lawnmower and really let your garden go to pieces. *(At this point, the man clutches his heart in agony and falls, dead, to the floor while the tape keeps waffling.)* Never again will you fall foul of the call of the chrysanthemum or the lure of the lupin, once you've bought 'How to overcome being an obsessive gardener'. And breathe out. Well done – your heart is now ready. In fact now YOU'RE ready – you're a new man! *(The man is in fact dead.)* Congratulations... doesn't it feel just great? Well, that's it. Thank you for buying this tape. Enjoy being a new man and remember... Yooouuu did it!!

1   What things about yourself do you like or not like?

2   Do you do anything to improve on your bad points or your good points? If so, what?

3   Do you ever turn to Jesus, or look in the Bible for help?

Psalm 139 (We are uniquely loved by God)

Luke 8:25–27 (Gaining the whole world but losing life)

A Funny Kind of Freedom

Edmund Farrow

THEMES: Freedom and rules / Being yourself

HANDY TIPS:

Props: *wallet; piece of paper for checklist.*

 2–3 minutes

CHARACTERS:

Trevor: a young man about to go on a first date. He is so stressed about making a good impression that he's probably eaten his odour-eaters and put toast in his shoes. He is wearing smart clothes but the effect is spoiled by a scruffy cardigan.

Trevor enters, checking he has cash in his wallet. He proceeds to centre stage and then faces the audience.

Trevor: Right, OK. *(He puts the wallet away and then concentrates on his watch.)* It's half past seven and I've got to meet her at the pictures at eight. It's a twenty minute walk and I should leave five minutes leeway, so, I'm OK – there's plenty of time. I just need to stay calm, stay calm. *(He paces up and down then halts suddenly.)* Checklist! *(He searches his pockets in panic and then finally pulls out a piece of paper).*

Right... right, checklist. OK. *(He begins to read his alternative Ten Commandments.)*

One: Deodorant. *(He smells his armpit.)* Check.

Two: Breath mints. *(He checks his pocket and then breathes into his hand to check he does not need a mint already.)* Check.

Three: Spots. Erm. *(He feels his face but is unsure.)* Mirror! *(He rushes across the stage and then mimes opening a door and looking in a mirror.)* Mirror. Aahhh. *(He relaxes and then panics. He has seen a spot.)* Argh! *(He pops it, mimes washing his face and then checks in the mirror again from all angles.)* Phew. *(He returns to centre stage.)*

Four: Clean socks. *(He looks at his feet and then contorts himself to sniff them.)* Oh well, close enough. Check.

Five: No sandals. Check. *(He starts to reel off the list more quickly.)*

Six: No dirt under fingernails. Check.

Seven: No cardigan. Ch... – Argh! *(He notices his cardigan and rips it off.)* I don't have time for this. I'm going to be late.

Eight: Think of four interesting things to talk about. Check.

Nine: Remember what they were. Er... *(He counts the things off on his fingers.)* The film... The weather... The political future of Europe and, er... *(He admits defeat.)* Star

Trek? *(He looks at the bit of paper.)* Drat! Oasis. I'm never going to get this right. *(He starts to bite his fingernails.)* She's bound to think I'm stupid or boring or something. No, no, stay calm. *(He takes a deep breath and smoothes himself down.)* Stay calm. *(He takes another deep breath.)*

Ten: Don't blow it. Right. That's it. OK, time to go. *(He throws away list and then grabs his coat. He walks to the edge of the stage, muttering under his breath.)* Film... Weather... The, er, the... *(He makes to retrieve the list but changes his mind.)* It's too late now. I have to go. Right. Stay calm. It's going to be fine. I just have to be myself, and she's bound to like me. *(He mimes opening a door and walks out, still counting on his fingers.)*

---

1   What is the purpose of having rules at all?

2   How do you feel when someone tells you what you should or shouldn't do?

3   Does freedom mean that you don't have any rules? In the light of the fact that Jesus has made us free, how should we react to some of the rules God has given us?

John 8:31,32 (The truth will set you free)

Jeremiah 31:33,34 (A new covenant: the law written on our hearts)

Galatians 3:10–14 (Righteousness does not come from observing the law)

BEST OF FRIENDS
Matt Sands

THEME: Easter / Peer pressure / Forgiveness

HANDY TIPS:

Props: *none necessary.*

 5 minutes

CHARACTERS:

Bog: sensible and fun. He cares strongly for his friend.

Bug: not so smart, and easily led. He ends up a loser but he's likeable.

This sketch is bright and funny, but it needs to switch dramatically to being more serious as it becomes a 'tragedy'. The main theme is the ongoing friendship between two kids who grew up the same way but became different, and who shared different eternities. The audience get to see Bug and Bog growing up and to laugh with them. As the sketch progresses they will age from children, through teenagers, to mature men. (If you have access to stage lighting, it might help to take the lights down between scenes.)

The two actors stand on-stage facing the audience. At the start of the sketch they are six-year-old boys. Their opening statements are bright and loud, and they behave as little kids on stage would do.

Bug: Hello everybody. My name is Bug. I'm six years old. I support Jerusalem United 'cos they're the champions. I have a dog called Noah and I have a best friend called Bog.

Bog: Hello my name is Bog. I am Bug's best friend. I am… (*he holds up eight fingers*) nearly six. My hobbies are football and fishing. I go to school every day with Bug.

Bug: Today we've been made to stay in after school because we've been naughty.

Bog: We've got to write 100 lines on why it was wrong to put that dead locust in Jennifer Refak's sandwich. *(Both boys are silent, then they begin to giggle.)* What have you put, Bug?

Bug: *(reading)* 'It was wrong to put the locust in Jennifer's sandwich because… the crunching noise of her chewing the sandwich ruined the peace of the lunch-hour.' *(He laughs.)*

Bog: Ha ha! I've put 'It was wrong because I hadn't put any mayonnaise in the sandwich first'. *(Both boys laugh.)*

Bug: We have real fun, me and Bog, 'cos we're…

Both: Best of friends. *(As they say this, they 'high ten', a high five with both hands.)*

Bog and Bug move around a bit and shake themselves. When they face the front again, it's years later.

Bog: We're fourteen now, and we've nearly finished school. Bug's still my best mate. I don't see him so much now cos he's going out with Jennifer. She must have a really short memory.

Bug: Wow, I'll be fifteen next week. Growing up goes a lot quicker than it used to. My mum died last year *(sadly)* and I don't see Dad much *(suddenly happy)*. But Bog's still about. I try and see as much of him as I can, but Jennifer's never forgotten when Bog put that locust in her school dinner that time.

They turn away again. It's a new scene and they're meeting up in the street.

Bog: Alright Bug!

Bug: Alright Bog!

Bog: So, it's Saturday night again mate. What do ya fancy doing? I hear some of the boys are going to wrap Pharisee Fred's house in toilet paper, if you're interested?

Bug: Nah, I can't make it tonight.

Bog: What!? But it's Saturday, Bug, it's our night.

Bug: Yeah I know… but Jennifer wants to see me and…

Bog: *(disappointed)* Oh… Jennifer. I should have known.

Bug: *(suddenly)* Not really sucker!! Ha ha… In fact if you look carefully here, I've got two tickets for United's game tonight as an early birthday present.

Bog: Wow!!

Bug: And who am I taking? Jennifer the Locust Breath? I think not. Who else but my lifelong companion and buddy, the Bog-man!!

Bog: Alright!! Wow!!

Bug: You really think I'd forget you that quick? I love you Bog.

Bog: I love you too Bug.

They embrace and hug, then catch the audience looking at them. They go all bashful, separate and begin to look at their nails, etc, trying to look manly. Then they laugh, turn to each other and slap a high ten again.

Both: Best of friends.

Some years later.

Bog: *(more serious now)* We're grown up now. Real men. I managed to do alright – I've got a job anyway, and a steady girlfriend. Still manage to go fishing once a week. Bug comes too... sometimes.

Bug: Things didn't go so well for me. I married Jennifer but she left pretty quick. I've got no job and I drink too much. Life ain't so good... *(brightens)* but I've still got Bog! Bog!

Bog: Bug!! *(They do a seriously fancy handshake.)* How are ya 'ma brudder'? Staying out of trouble? Fancy some fishing tonight?

Bug: Yeah mate, the fishing's cool. But I need your help with a little something first.

Bog: Just name it mate... wanna send Jen some more locusts?

Bug: Nah. I just need to pay a quick visit to someone's house. Someone who's not in.

Bog: *(not happy, realising Bug wants to burgle a house)* Bug. Don't get me involved again mate... I'm doin' alright.

Bug: Yeah, but I'm not. Please Bog, it's a rich old bloke's house. I know he's not there 'cos he's up in the hills listening to the carpenter from Nazareth. It's just a quick in-and-out.

Bog: Is this the same Jesus who says it's wrong to steal? The miracle man who talks about love instead of hate?

Bug: Look, this is the last time, I promise...

I'll never ask again. But I'm desperate Bog... and after all, we are... best of friends?

Bug offers up his hands for a high ten. Bog pauses to think and then commits to the slap. As their hands collide, they freeze for a few seconds, and then slowly the two friends step backwards and take up a crucifixion stance. They have become the two thieves crucified on either side of Jesus.

Bog: Bug got it wrong. The old man was in. He was, in fact, quite a surprise. And so here I am, dying with my friend.

Bug: It wasn't supposed to happen like this. Nothing was. So how come I'm here, being crucified? *(He turns his head towards centre stage, where Jesus would be.)* Hey, Jesus. You're the man with all the answers. Save yourself, and us.

Bog: Don't say that Bug... we deserve what we're getting. But he's done nothing wrong. *(He turns to Jesus.)* Jesus, remember me when you get to your kingdom.

The characters freeze, and then Bug quietly exits. Bog takes up a lone position centre stage. He is looking around.

Bog: Well, Jesus was right. This is paradise. It's amazing... and I can't really begin to understand how I got here. It's incredible... but Bug's not here. He couldn't come. It's weird being without him... I keep expecting him to jump out on me, but he doesn't. Things didn't work as we expected. But I'll never forget him... We really were the best of friends.

1   What things have you done because someone else influenced you (ie personal friends, media)?

2   What is more important: helping a friend or doing what you think is right? Why?

3   If we find ourselves in a situation where we realise that we've done the wrong thing, what should we do?

4   Does forgiveness from God mean that we don't face any of the consequences of our actions?

Luke 23:32–43 (The two thieves crucified with Jesus)

CUBBY MACGREGOR

Matt Sands

THEME: Healing / Being different / Prejudice

HANDY TIPS:

Props: *two chairs; a mug; sunglasses.*

 4 minutes

CHARACTERS:

Narrator A: a sensible and happy lady.

Narrator B: a happy, cheeky chap, he has no sense of propriety.

Cubby MacGregor: the blind man. He doesn't say anything but just goes with the flow.

Jesus: in control. Son of God. Say no more.

The two narrators stand on chairs six feet apart and speak to the audience.

The narrative (in bold) is poetic, so they need to maintain some sort of beat, and their in-between bits (in normal type) are just 'asides' to show they are real. Cubby and Jesus energetically act out the story in mime.

Cubby stands in front of the narrators holding out an empty mug in one hand and sunglasses in the other. He is looking straight ahead.

A: **This is the story of Cubby MacGregor.**

B: **Cubby MacGregor was a dirty old beggar.**

Both: **You're a dirty old beggar, Cubby MacGregor.**

A: **Forced into begging as a means to an end.**

B: Poor old Cubby, he's got no friends.

A: He lives in a box down a dirty old street,

B: With a public health warning attached to his feet.

(*shouting to Cubby, aside from the narrative*) Cos they're a bit smelly, aren't they Cubby? In fact, you're quite smelly aren't you? (*The narrator looks pleased with himself.*)

A: Despite this, a nicer bloke you never would find.

B: Cubby's big problem is he's totally blind.

(*Cubby puts on dark glasses*) Oh. (*He stops and looks at A.*)

A: What's up?

B: If I'd known he was blind I would never have made fun of him. Now I feel awful.

A: Serves you right.

Anyway, one day Cubby was particularly broke.

B: (*trying to make up for it*) **You know, Cubby is a smashing bloke**.

A: Get on with it. Don't try and be funny.

B: Come here Cubby, I'll give you some money. (*He drops a coin in Cubby's cup.*)

A: Feel better now? Can I get on with the story?

B: OK, OK. 'Jackanory... Jackanory.'

A: Cubby and freedom are about to collide,

B: For along came a man who stopped by his side. (*Enter Jesus.*)

A: Told Cubby his name – said it was Jesus.

B: (*pause*) Nothing rhymes with Jesus! What am I supposed to say, 'gave him some Maltesers' or something?

A: Alright, don't worry. The good bit is coming up soon.

The man looked at Cubby and his heart filled with love.

B: And he knew this was why he'd been sent from above.

A: Then as he spoke to the crowd, the gauntlet was hurled.

B: Jesus pointed his finger, said 'I'm the light of the world.'

Jesus now follows the narrative with his actions. At this point the two narrators look at each other and react to the events, clapping and rubbing their hands together as it gets exciting.

A: (*slowly*) **Jesus spat on the ground and mixed in some mud,**

B: So the ends of his fingers were covered in crud.

A: He said, 'That looks good, I'll try it for size.'

B: Stood up and rubbed it in Cubby's eyes.

A: Eucch! That's gross... soil and saliva.

B: Hmmm. Not your conventional eyedrops that's for sure.

A: Cubby looked stupid and felt like a fool.

B: Jesus just smiled and said, 'Wash in the pool.'

A: As he washed in the water, a glimmer of light,

B: A shape and a colour appeared in his sight.

A: He jumped to his feet and cried out with glee,

B: *(exaltantly)* For Cubby MacGregor, the beggar could see!

Cubby cries out, and the narrators jump down excitedly and do a little jig. They then get back on their chairs. Cubby and Jesus have also embraced.

A: It's a miracle!!

B: Yep. The world's first signs and wonders face pack. The women will be queuing up for them!

A: Let's finish up.

Cubby cried, 'Master, now I'm complete,'

B: 'But what can you do for me smelly old feet?'

A: With his arm around Cubby, Jesus said, 'Follow me.'

B: 'I'll follow,' said Cubby, 'because now I can see.'

Jesus and Cubby exit. B jumps down and walks out with them.

A: Hey, where are you going?

B: I'm going with them.

A: But your line...

B: Oh, you do it. *(A shrugs shoulders.)*

A: So that was the story of Cubby MacGregor,

No longer a smelly and dirty old beggar,

Whose darkness was taken and far away hurled,

By one man who said 'I'm the light of the world.'

1 How do we personally, or our society in general, relate to people who are underprivileged?

2 How do we feel about being unconventional or going against the flow?

3 Do we do all the things that Jesus did? If not, why not?

 John 9:1–11 (Jesus heals the man born blind)

ME

Matt Sands

THEME: The gospel / What's life all about? / The love of God

HANDY TIPS:

Props: *Costumes are vital to present the characters in a credible way. They should be dressed as follows:*
Tarzan in a jungle outfit or camouflage trousers, and bare chested;
Bazza in football strip and holding a football;
Al-Sharif in linens, Arab head attire and huge sunglasses;
Crystal in posh clothes, lots of jewellery and with a cigarette;
Jesus ... well, whatever you think appropriate!

 4 minutes

CHARACTERS:

Tarzan: simple and in his own world.

Bazza: a footballer – one of the lads and proud. Despite being a footie-god, he is plain and looks pretty normal.

Al-Sharif: An oil-rich sheikh – greedy and seedy. He won't give much away and is very uncaring. Life, for him, is a liveable fantasy.

Crystal: She is a very important character, designed to touch our hearts through her very real hurt behind the plastic image. You wish she could just be herself, but the world has already ruined her.

Jesus: Our loving, supremely different friend and father. There's also a challenge in his speech.

This is a simple presentation, and is not hard to learn, but the key to it working is to present the characters to the audience with as much meaning as possible. It can be performed anywhere, and is straightforward, funny, heart-touching gospel.

The characters are lined up along the stage, facing the audience. They deliver their lines one after the other.

Tarzan: Me Tarzan, king of the jungle.

Bazza: Me Bazza, king of Wembley.

Al: Me Al-Sharif, sheikh of El-abba-land.

Crystal: Me Crystal, queen of Hollywood.

Jesus: Me Jesus, king of the Jews.

Pause.

Tarzan: Me Tarzan, have a girlfriend called Jane.

Bazza: Me Bazza, got a bird named... Spice Girl!

Al: Me Al-Sharif, have sixteen wives, called one to sixteen.

Crystal: Me Crystal, have a stunningly rich boyfriend called... *(forgets, pulls out huge list which unrolls almost to the floor)* Oh yes, Forbes.

Jesus: Me Jesus, I'm just in love with everyone.

Pause.

Tarzan: Me Tarzan, hang about with the animals.

Bazza: Me Bazza, well I hang about wiv the lads, don't I?!

Al: Me Al-Sharif, hang about with dollar bills *(pulling a wad from his pocket).*

Crystal: *(seeing Al's money)* Me Crystal, hang about with Mr Al-Sharif. *(She smiles and takes his arm.)*

Jesus: Me Jesus, hang about with beggars and sick people, or anyone who needs me.

Pause.

Tarzan: Me Tarzan, son of wolves and monkeys.

Bazza: Me Bazza, son of Mr & Mrs A Smith, 11 Stockton Rd, Salford.

Al: Me Al-Sharif, son of father and number twenty-two.

Crystal: *(looks sad)* Me Crystal, don't know who I'm the daughter of.

Jesus: Me Jesus, Son of God, Father of all.

Pause.

Tarzan: Me Tarzan, give protection from headhunters.

Bazza: Me Bazza, give you twenty goals a season.

Al: Me Al-Sharif, give you nothing.

Crystal: Me Crystal, give you anything.

Jesus: Me Jesus, give you everything.

Pause.

Tarzan: Me Tarzan, nailed together a new tree house.

Bazza: Me Bazza, nailed by the manager for a lousy game.

Al: *(looking disgusted)* Me Al-Sharif, nailed by my accountant.

Crystal: *(looking ashamed)* Me Crystal, nailed by everyone.

Jesus: Me Jesus, nailed by my hands and feet.

Pause.

Tarzan: Me Tarzan, need a new loincloth.

Bazza: Me Bazza, need a new haircut.

Al: Me Al-Sharif, need a new oil field.

Crystal: Me Crystal, need therapy.

Jesus: Me Jesus, I need you.

Pause.

Tarzan: Me Tarzan, going back to jungle. *(Exits.)*

Bazza: Me Bazza, off down the boozer. *(Exits.)*

Al: Me Al-Sharif, going to smoke hash in my limousine. *(Exits.)*

Crystal: Me Crystal, going to waste. *(She just looks at the floor.)*

Jesus: Me Jesus, staying right here. *(To audience.)* Where are you going?

All freeze.

---

1 What are your plans for your life?

2 What kind of person do you think you are? What kind of person would you like to be?

3 Can Jesus make a difference to your life?

Titus 3:3–7 (God's kindness and love towards us)

SPIRITUAL LESSONS

Edmund Farrow

THEMES: More to life than flesh and blood / Thinking about the spiritual realm / God's involvement in our day to day life/ The work of the Holy Spirit

HANDY TIPS:

Props: *thermos flask; cup; chair; blanket for Jason.*

 4–5 minutes

CHARACTERS:

Leonara: a senior angelic field operative who knows her stuff but who has probably been around humans just a tiny bit too long. She seems lax at first but, in reality, she is still a razor-sharp member of the Heavenly Host. Her contact with humanity has mellowed her, rather than corrupted her.

Drimble: a bit dim for a warrior of light, really, but he is eager to serve and to learn. He needs to want to care and to serve more than he wants to fight.

Jason: a very sound sleeper.

The two angels should be wearing similar, plain clothing, such as jeans and white T-shirts. Tinsel haloes or something similar might also be a good idea in order to make it obvious who they are (just as long as it doesn't look too silly).

Leonara is sitting on a chair, sipping tea from a thermos and watching over the sleeping form of Jason, who is lying in front of her. Drimble, a lower-ranking angel enters and tries to attract her attention.

Drimble: Excuse me, ma'am.

Leonara: What? *(She notices the other angel for the first time. Drimble salutes smartly and Leonara acknowledges it more casually.)* Oh, I didn't see you there, soldier. Drimble, isn't it? What are you doing here?

Drimble: You are required in the heavenly city, ma'am. I am to relieve you of your duty guarding this human, ma'am.

Leonara: Fair enough. *(She stands up and collects her things together.)* Take care of him, he's not such a bad lad really. He's a bit confused at times but God's in his heart, and that's what counts. *(She starts to walk off.)* Right, be seeing you...

Drimble: *(anxiously)* Er... ma'am?

Leonara: *(pausing in her exit)* Yes?

Drimble: Er, what do I have to do?

Leonara: *(sighing)* Well, you can knock off this 'ma'am' business for a start. We're all angels together down here. *(She walks back towards him.)* Now, what do you think you're supposed to do? *(Drimble stands to attention, eyes to the front.)*

Drimble: *(with assurance)* Guard.

Leonara: Yep.

Drimble: Serve.

Leonara: Yep.

Drimble: Protect.

Leonara: Yep. *(She smiles and moves to congratulate Drimble but frowns as he continues.)*

Drimble: And...

Leonara: *(disconcertingly)* And?

Drimble: *(nervously)* And give the occasional piece of advice?

Leonara: *(She glares at him.)* No. I wouldn't do that if I were you, soldier. Do you know what it's like being human?

Drimble: *(whimpering)* No.

Leonara: *(She glares at Drimble for a moment longer and then relents and relaxes.)* No, neither do I. After all these years, I'm beginning to get an idea but I suggest you leave the advice to someone more qualified.

Drimble: *(puzzled)* Ma'am?

Leonara: You know. *(She points upwards.)*

Drimble: *(getting the hint)* Oh.

Leonara: Yes, exactly. Anyway, I suppose, seeing as I'm delayed already, I might as well fill you in on what's been happening to Jason recently. A guy called Mike has been trying to pick a fight with him for ages. Yesterday, he told Jason that he had big ears, a big nose and spots.

Drimble: *(peering closely at Jason.)* He does.

Leonara: *(slightly miffed)* Well yes, but the truth hurts sometimes, you know. Anyway, it was a virtual textbook case of turning the other cheek. The Spirit told him to shrug it off and walk away.

Drimble: Did he?

Leonara: Nah. He went for the right hook. *(She demonstrates.)* Bam! He's in no end of trouble.

Drimble: *(despondently)* Great.

Leonara: No, no, it's better that way. It gives the Master more room to work. Next time the outcome could be quite different.

Drimble: How is that?

Leonara: Let me give you another example. The other week, Jason, here, was having difficulty with demons.

Drimble: *(looking about in panic)* What? In fighting them off?

Leonara: No. In believing in them.

Drimble: *(confused)* Sorry? How could he not believe in demons? That's... that's like not believing in us.

Leonara: *(shrugging)* Well, that's humans for you - blind to what they can't see.

Drimble: *(His lips move as he thinks that one over.)* Erm.

Leonara: Look, anyway, the Spirit set to work making things clear in Jason's mind. For the entire week, every Christian he met had a sudden urge to talk to him about spiritual warfare. Other people told him about spooky experiences they'd had. Relevant Bible passages just seemed to attract his attention, and then, finally, he came home one night and switched on the X-Files. There was this possessed kid...

Drimble: *(getting very excited)* I saw it! There was this kid and people kept dying and Sculley didn't believe a word of it but Mulder did and they had an exorcism and,

and ectoplasm sprayed everywhere. It was really cool!

Leonara: *(pointedly)* Biblically inaccurate on a number of counts, of course.

Drimble: *(remembering himself)* Oh, er, yes, of course.

Leonara: Anyway, as I was saying, Jason suddenly had a lot to think about. The Spirit has all kinds of ways of guiding and instructing. And that's only part of his job.

Drimble: Yes, but what do I have to do?

Leonara: Stand guard and not get ideas above your station, soldier. *(She turns to leave again.)*

Drimble: *(snapping back to attention)* Yes, ma'am.

Leonara: *(She turns back briefly.)* Oh, and, soldier...

Drimble: Ma'am?

Leonara: Never forget how much the Master loves him. If you do that, you won't go far wrong.

Drimble: Yes, ma'am.

Leonara exits and Drimble takes up position behind Jason. They freeze.

1   Do you believe in angels, demons and the spiritual realm?

2   Do you think about them too much or too little in your life?

3   How do you understand or think about the Holy Spirit

4   Think back over your life. Can you see any examples of how God (the Holy Spirit) has been working?

John 14:16,17 (The Holy Spirit: who he is and what he does)

John 16:7–15

1 Corinthians 12:1–11

Hebrews 1:14 (Some information on angels)

Ephesians 6:10–12 (Being aware of the spiritual battle we face)

FOR GOD SO LOVED THE WORLD
(HE DIDN'T SEND A COMMITTEE)
Edmund Farrow

THEME: Easter / Compromising the gospel / Evangelism

HANDY TIPS:

Props: *calculator; a ring-binder for each character; a long table; six chairs.*

 7–8 minutes

CHARACTERS:

Jane: A businesslike, executive type who does not suffer fools gladly. She is the chairperson of the meeting.

Helena: The commissar for political correctness. She is a bit of an amateur psychologist and is very much into 'the needs of the audience'. Her tone of voice is reasoned and concerned, but her actual words are rubbish.

George: George is a cautious accountant who fiddles with a calculator as much as with the script.

Rachel: The girl is just not quite all there. She doodles and stares off into space. She keeps turning the pages of her script in the wrong direction. She often sighs in a 'It's a sunny day... what am I doing here?' kind of way. She is, in other words, a complete space cadet.

Steve: Steve is a teeny bit excitable. He is an epic maker trapped in a room full of Philistines and penny-pinchers. He uses wild hand movements and apocalyptic tones just to ask for a cup of tea, so if he really wants to make an impact, it's best to get out of the way.

Jackie: The token sensible person on the committee. (There's always one!) She doesn't particularly like contradicting the others, but it all becomes a bit much for her in the end. Luckily, she seldom gets a word in.

OK, people, it's a script writers' meeting to discuss the latest biblical blockbuster. There is a table centre stage with Helena sitting at one end. George, Rachel, Jackie and Steve sit in that order behind the table, facing the audience. They are chatting amongst themselves as the sketch starts. Jane enters with a pile of papers and sits down opposite Helena. All the characters have ring-binders, containing 'scripts' of the programme, which they flick through at the appropriate moment.

Jane: Right, let's get down to business, people. Glad to see you all made it and I hope you're all brimming over with ideas. We've got a lot to get through today. As you know, shooting starts in three days time and we need to have the script locked up tight by then. Ken has mentioned a few things he has problems with and there are some others I've been thinking over. The most pressing is, of course, that we still need a title for the production.

George: The Life and Times of Jesus.

Jane: Accurate but boring.

Steve: From Carpenter to King – One Man's Story of a Struggle Against Oppression and...

Jane: *(cutting him dead)* No.

Helena: Jesus of Nazareth.

Jane: Been done.

Rachel: Little House on the Prairie.

There is a pause while everyone looks strangely at Rachel.

Jane: Rachel, are you feeling OK?

Rachel: Sorry, just thinking aloud.

Steve: Scary.

Jackie: Son of God – as the title I mean. 'Son of God'.

Jane: Sounds too much like a sequel.

Jackie: Well, what about 'God' then?

Jane: Yes! I like it! 'Well, what about God then?' – it has a certain ring to it.

Jackie: That's not...

George: It has great merchandising potential! T-shirts, badges, lunch boxes, bumper stickers...

Steve: Yes, that question mark is really in-your-face punctuation. What a concept!

Jane: OK, that's sorted out. Well done, Jackie. Now, moving on. Look at page twenty-five. The Pharisees have brought a woman caught in adultery.

Helena: An alternative lifestyle. We don't want to offend the monogamously-challenged in the audience.

Jane: Thank you, Helena, yes you're right. OK, as I was saying, the Pharisees have brought this woman before Jesus and said that she deserves to die. He says to let whoever hasn't done anything wrong, throw the first stone. The tension mounts, the rocks are poised – and then they all just wander off. Jesus tells the woman to go and not sin again. What an anti-climax. Surely we can do better than that, people.

Jackie: But isn't he implying that...

George: How about the disciples leaping out of the bushes...

Jane: With drawn swords...

Steve: On motorbikes! I can see it now! *(Steve leaps up and moves round the room, sweeping his arms to demonstrate the scene.)* The roar of the engines, the screams of the Pharisees, the howl of a descending pillar of fire and then, amidst all the mayhem, Jesus turns to the woman, his hair and clothes billowing in the gale. He raises his arm *(Steve points out into the audience)* and he says, 'I want YOU for a sunbeam'. What do you think? *(There is a pause.)*

Helena: It has potential. *(Most of the others murmur and nod. Steve sits down again.)*

George: It's not going to be cheap... and I'm not too sure about the motorbikes.

Jane: Yes, perhaps we could do with slightly less of a climax but, er, something to look into. Moving on... Helena, you were telling me something about the 'I am the bread of life' line.

Helena: Yes, I was wondering if we could change it to attract a more affluent audience. We have plenty of social justice rhetoric earlier on, that I feel some people may have problems identifying with. Perhaps 'I am the croissant of life' would be better for the purposes of balance. Something for the home counties.

George: Might be good for our advertising revenue.

Jane: Yes, perhaps we can...

Rachel: What about all the sheep?

Another pause and yet more disbelief.

Jane: Is something troubling you, Rachel?

Rachel: I'm just thinking we're going to need some sheep. Jesus keeps describing himself as a good shepherd. Perhaps he ought to have a chance to show it.

George: I'm not sure we can stretch the budget to a sheepdog trial.

Helena: It would appeal to the animal-lovers in the audience. I'm not sure their needs have been addressed anywhere else, as yet.

Jackie: I think we might possibly be missing the point here.

Steve: No, no, we have to consider these things. You need to grasp the true majesty of the entire project – how the little details build up to produce an epic production. Why should we stop with sheep? Let's have antelopes, giraffes... elephants!

Jane: Calm down Steve, before George has a stroke. A few sheep – maybe. Anything else is out of the question. Right, let's get back to the agenda. On page thirty, Jesus talks about his followers not seeing death. I think we can safely lose that one. Oh, and just on from there, he says, 'I have come that they may have life and have it to the full.'

George: Seems a bit unlikely, doesn't it? Considering what kind of life he had.

Helena: Yes, and what does he know about the aspirations of the late twentieth-century individual?

Jackie: Well, quite a lot actually.

Helena: We need to make the entire programme more relevant to the spirit of the times.

Jackie: Oh, for goodness' sake...

Jane: Well, I think losing the line will be fine for now. All those in favour... *(All except Jackie raise their hands.)* Right, that's settled. Anything else before we have a break?

George: Actually, can I bring something up?

Jane: That depends. *(She looks at her watch.)*

George: Well, we've had a crew of twenty-five building the temple set for three weeks and it's still not finished. And on page fourteen we've got Jesus saying, 'Destroy this temple and I will raise it again in three days.' I reckon it would have taken him at least a year.

Rachel: He was a carpenter.

George: OK, call it nine months.

Jackie: I think he was talking about himself and the resurrection and stuff. He sort of ties it in later with the 'I am the Resurrection and the Life' line.

Jane: Ah, sorry, I meant to tell you – we cut that out at the last meeting when you weren't here.

Jackie: But that's a good line.

Jane: No, not the line – the resurrection scene.

Jackie: What? *(She flicks to the end of her script.)*

Steve: Yes, we thought it would be a lot more poignant if we left it with the burial.

George: Not to mention cheaper.

Helena: Yes, and the viewers will be able to empathise better – it's much more symbolic of the angst inherent in the modern mind.

Jackie: Hang on, you've got Peter running off with Mary Magdalene and starting up a kibbutz by the Sea of Galilee. That's not what happens in the book.

Rachel: I just love a happy ending.

Jackie: It had a happy ending already!

George: It just wasn't very marketable.

Helena: Yes, we have to set some limit to the audience's ability to suspend disbelief.

Jackie: But he did make all those claims...

Jane: I'm sorry, Jackie, but it's too late now. If you have a problem, take it up with the producer. Right, thanks very much, people. I think this is going to be a stupendous programme – you can all congratulate yourselves. Now, let's have some coffee.

They all exit, remaining in character.

1   Do you believe some bits of the Bible and not others?

2   When you're talking to someone about Jesus, do you emphasise some bits of the gospel and not others? If so, why is that?

3   How easy is it to stand up for something you believe when everyone around you believes something different?

4   What would make it easier?

2 Timothy 4:1–5 (Encouragement to preach the gospel)

Galatians 1:6–9 (Distorting the gospel)

LIGHTS OUT

Tony Bower

THEME: To show Christians our responsibility to be a light in this world / Why we should evangelise

HANDY TIPS:

Props: *a lightbulb; a few fun props to suggest having been in the sea, ie plastic fish, shells, seaweed.*

 3 minutes

CHARACTERS:

Lighthouse keeper: he is completely oblivious to the state the ship's captain is in.

Ship's captain: he is wet, tired and angry.

The ship's captain walks up to the lighthouse keeper, absolutely fuming. He mimes being dripping wet and stands glaring at the lighthouse keeper.

Lighthouse keeper: Excuse me, is something wrong?

Ship's captain: *(spluttering)* Wrong? Wrong? Wrong?

Lighthouse keeper: You seem a little upset.

Ship's captain: Upset? Upset? Upset?

Lighthouse keeper: You've not swallowed some parrot seed have you?

Ship's captain: Don't be so ridiculous. You should *know* why I'm upset. You should *know* what's wrong.

Lighthouse keeper: Sorry, you've got me there. Haven't got a clue.

Ship's captain: I'm a ship's captain.

Lighthouse keeper: Congratulations. Pleased to meet you. *(He shakes his hand.)*

Ship's captain: And... (*He points to himself.*)

Lighthouse keeper: And... you've been for a swim?

Ship's captain: You are a lighthouse keeper, are you not?

Lighthouse keeper: Yes, I am.

Ship's captain: (*working himself into a Basil Fawlty-like state of anger and sarcasm*) Well, do you mind if I ask you a question? I mean you may think it is such a little thing to ask... so trivial... hardly worth mentioning in fact, but I would like to ask, if it's alright?

Lighthouse keeper: Go ahead.

Ship's captain: Why is the light not on?

Lighthouse keeper: Because I switched it off.

Ship's captain: You did *what*? Sorry, I must have got some seaweed in my ears. I thought you said you had switched it off.

Lighthouse keeper: That's right. Look, let me show you. (*He grabs hold of the ship's captain.*) That lever is for 'on', that one for 'off'. Well I pulled *that* one. (*He points to the 'off' lever.*)

Ship's captain: But this is a *light*house. You are a lighthouse *keeper*. It's your job, your responsibility, to shine the light.

Lighthouse keeper: I know and I do.

Ship's captain: You do?

Lighthouse keeper: One day a week. (*He mimes switching it on.*) Oh, and it does look lovely, especially on a dark night. You can see it for miles. Ships love it – it's so comforting to know it's there.

Ship's captain: I'm sure they do. So would we. So why does it only shine once a week?

Lighthouse keeper: The cost.

Ship's captain: The cost?

Lighthouse keeper: These bulbs aren't cheap you know. (*He shows him a small bulb.*) See this bulb?

Ship's captain: That doesn't look expensive.

Lighthouse keeper: It's not. Our light bulbs are nothing like this. Much bigger, much brighter, much more costly.

Ship's captain: (*in disbelief*) You only shine the light one day a week?

Lighthouse keeper: Sometimes we shine it on special occasions. The QE2 came past one day... we shone it all night. Lovely ship!

Ship's captain: So apart from special occasions, the light is only switched on one day a week, because of the cost.

Lighthouse keeper: That's right.

Ship's captain: Have you thought what would happen if a ship was sailing out at sea on a very dark and stormy night, like this one for instance... get the picture? (*The lighthouse keeper nods and begins to sway gently.*) Suddenly the storm begins to increase, waves lash over the side of the boat, the ship is going up and down, up and down... *(The lighthouse keeper goes to be sick.)* What are you doing?

Lighthouse keeper: I feel sick.

Ship's captain: Just supposing this ship, out there on a stormy night like this one, is looking for the harbour, but there's no light shining to warn them of the nasty rocks and no way of being able to see them. Now here's the question: what do you think will happen?

Lighthouse keeper: The ship will crash.

Ship's captain: Yes, it would crash! And you'd have to swim to shore in freezing water, feeling like you were going to drown, choking on seaweed. Now, now do you know why I'm angry?

Lighthouse keeper: No.

The ship's captain faints.

---

1 What things inspire you to tell others about them (ie TV programmes, music, a football match)? Why?

2 Is it important to tell people about what Jesus has done? Why?

Matthew 5:14–16 ('Let your light shine before men...')

John 8:12 (Jesus – the light of the world)

Proverbs 4:18,19 (Walking in the light)

THE FINE

Tony Bower

THEMES: The concept of sin / Punishment / Justice

HANDY TIPS:

Props: *a piece of paper to represent a parking ticket; a pad and pencil for the traffic warden.*

 3 minutes

CHARACTERS:

Woman

Traffic warden

A traffic warden is walking casually down the street with a notepad and pen in hand. Now and again he stops and writes something in the pad, then continues on his way. A woman rushes up to the traffic warden, out of breath and clutching a ticket.

Woman: Did you give me this? *(She has thrust the ticket in his face whilst he is trying to write. Slowly he reads the ticket.)*

Traffic warden: Yes, I believe I did.

Woman: What on earth do you think you were playing at?

Traffic warden: I wasn't playing at anything madam. I was doing my job.

He hands her back the ticket and continues on his way. The woman stares at him in disbelief. She runs to catch him up again and stands in front of him.

Woman: And that's it, is it?

Traffic warden: Pardon?

Woman: You're just going to give me this ticket and walk off, are you?

Traffic warden: Yes!

The woman looks indignant.

Woman: Don't you realise I was only parked illegally for two minutes? Doesn't that count for something? Don't you take that into consideration?

Traffic warden: No.

Woman: Some of my friends park on double yellow lines all the time.

Traffic warden: Tut, tut!

Woman: Would you believe me if I said this was the first time I had parked on double yellow lines?

Traffic warden: Yes, I would.

Woman: So does that make any difference?

Traffic warden: No.

Woman: No?

Traffic warden: I am very sorry madam but the law is the law. If you break it, it's broken, even if you do it just the once for a few seconds.

Woman: Well, what about my friends?

Traffic warden: I thought we were talking about your fine, madam.

Woman: ... umph.

Traffic warden: Madam?

Woman: Yes?

Traffic warden: You have removed your car, haven't you?

Woman: Well, I er... intend to, of course... straight away, but I thought I would try to talk to you first.

Traffic warden: Oh dear.

Woman: Oh dear?

Traffic warden: My colleague came on duty about five minutes ago.

He looks down the road. The woman looks horrified and runs off. The traffic warden waves, shouts goodbye, shakes his head and continues with his work.

1   Did the person deserve to be fined? Does the fact that it was her first offence make any difference?

2   Are some crimes worse than others? How do you think God views the things we do wrong?

Romans 3:23,24 (We all fall short of the glory of God)

Amazing Stories

Matt Sands

THEME: What do you believe? / Can we believe what Jesus said? / Is the Bible true?

HANDY TIPS:

Props: *a table; two pint glasses; a small book to repesent the Gospel of John.*

 4 minutes

CHARACTERS:

Bill and Bob: both sorry non-intellectuals with very gullible minds, but exceptionally likeable.

This is an easy-to-do sketch, relying on comic exaggeration and two amiable characters. Bill and Bob spend the entire sketch simply sitting at a table in a pub, trying to outdo each other with absurd stories. As they recant these tales, they need to be really animated and convinced of what they're saying. These men are mad (and the sketch is just as bad...), so feel free to really ham it up!

Bill: Alright then, Bob?

Bob: Alright then, Bill?

Bill: How d'you do today then?

Bob: Ooh, I made about five hundred smackers, I reckon. Not a bad day at all.

Bill: Good, Bob, not bad. *(He pauses to sip his beer.)*

Bob: How's the missus, Bill?

Bill: Fine, Bob. At home watching Coronation Street.

Bob: Say no more. Quality television.

Bill: That's right... fine entertainment.

Pause again.

Bob: I was watching something interesting earlier meself, Bill. Fascinating programme about people overcoming natural disaster. They had this bloke on, right, and his plane crash-landed in the middle of the Sahara desert. He's stranded, two thousand miles from civilisation. He's there for five days with no food or drink, crawling over these huge sand dunes, and just as he's about to drop dead, guess what he finds?

Bill: (*intrigued*) What?

Bob: An abandoned Coca-Cola factory, still stocked with thousands of cans.

Bill: What – in the middle of the Sahara?

Bob: I swear mate, it's true! He drank about five hundred cans of Coke, and then, do you know what else he found in the factory? Another light aeroplane, exactly like the one that he'd crashed, and he flew all the way back home, and he's perfectly alright.

Bill: Cor, that's amazing!

Bob: Lucky geezer, eh?

Bill: Amazing Bob, amazing!

They pause for a drink.

You know Bob, that reminds me of a story I read in a magazine recently. This bloke is walking his dog in this field on a Sunday afternoon, when all of a sudden this spacecraft the size of Wembley Stadium lands in front of him. This green man with four heads comes out, points a laser gun at the dog, shoots it and guess what it turned into?

Bob: What?

Bill: A chicken.

Bob: Never!

Bill: On me life mate! Then the spacecraft takes off, and this bloke is left standing beside a chicken, which can now strangely speak eight different languages.

Bob: Cor! The things that can happen nowadays.

Bill: You can't depend on anything, can ya?

Bob: You can't Bill, you can't. I mean the flaming cheek of it... I mean, who do these little green men think they are?

Bill: Martians, I presume Bob.

Bob: Yeah, but it's right up front, eh Bill? I mean, turning some guy's dog into a chicken... that's terrible! I mean, who ever heard of the phrase, 'a man's best friend is his chicken'?

Bill: You're right Bobby-boy – those Martians should be banished from the face of the earth.

Another pause.

Bob: Well, if you think that's amazing then get your lugholes around this pukka little ditty. In the paper this morning was this story about a man who's had enough, so he jumps off a cliff. It just so happens that the Women's Olympic trampolining team are practising on the beach below. He's swept by a gust of wind onto the trampoline below, catapulted four hundred feet back into the air and gets snagged on the wheels of a hijacked jumbo jet passing overhead. The jumbo crash-lands in Libya where he's mistaken for a spy, is sentenced to death and then rescued from the gallows by that same spaceman who turned the dog into a chicken... and he was still back in time for the match on telly that evening.

Bill: Never!

Bob: Straight up, mate!

Bill: Where d'you read that then, *The Sun*?

Bob: Nah, mate, *The Times* I think it was.

Pause.

Bill: Yes Bob, that is truly amazing, but lean your listening regalia round this trim little tale. I read in this book, OK, that there's this bloke and he's got five thousand hungry people gathered around him. They're all starving and want some food. You know what happened?

Bob: Nope... tell me.

Bill: All he's got is two small fish and five loaves of bread. He breaks 'em up, puts 'em in a basket and passes it round, and there was enough to feed all five thousand people until they're full.

They pause in silence, and then both break out in hysterical laughter.

Bob: Cor, the things people expect you to believe!

Bill: I know mate, I know!

Bob: Next you're gonna tell me there was some left over.

Bill: There was! There was!

Absolute raucous laughter.

Bob: *(wipes tears from his eyes)* What sort of book did you read that in then?

Bill: Oh, it was some little red book, called John I think it was.

Bob: Cor, they'd make anything up nowadays. Well, I'm off home mate... there's a decent programme on later about the Abominable Snowman. I'll be seeing ya!

Bob exits.

Bill: Yeah, see ya Bob.

He sits quietly at the table and pulls the Gospel of John out of his pocket. He looks at it and chuckles.

Cor, that really had me going for a moment then.

He tosses the Bible onto the table and exits.

1   Do you believe all you hear?

2   What makes you decide to believe something (ie the source of the information, background knowledge)?

3   How much of what's written in the Bible do you believe?

2 Timothy 3:16 (The reliability of the Bible)

2 Peter 1:16–21

THE BUNGEE JUMP

Matt Sands

THEME: Faith

HANDY TIPS:

Props: *none necessary.*

 3–4 minutes

CHARACTERS:

A: The bungee man. He's calm and secretly enjoying himself at the jumper's expense.

B: The jumper. He's sharp but scared. He has no idea what a bungee jump is, and doesn't want to risk losing his (very comfortable) life.

The two characters are at the top of a bungee jump. At the end of the sketch, one jumps, so a raised stage is needed. (Alternatively one will have to roll around on the floor, simulating a fall... but it works!). No props are needed, just good comic timing. If a short talk is to follow the sketch, try and keep it light-hearted, but relevant.

Oh, and as a warning: you may want to check with someone in charge about the last line of the sketch. Incredibly some people still find words like 'naked' a bit taboo for church. (Yes, I know Jesus said it but...).

The two characters are on stage. One appears to be tying something around the other man's ankles.	**B:** OK, so what do I do?
	A: Well... you jump!
A: There you go sir, you're ready to do your first bungee jump.	**B:** Jump? *(He jumps a few inches on the spot.)* OK, and then?

A: No sir, you jump off there. *(He points off the front of the stage.)*

B: *(Looks and jumps back horrified.)* ARE YOU MAD??!!

A: But sir...

B: I'm not jumping off there – I'll kill myself. You must be completely bonkers!

A: No sir, that's the whole idea. You jump off the platform into the ravine.

B: *(incredulous)* INTO THE RAVINE??! But I'll die!

A: No you won't. The rubber bands around your legs will pull you back just before impact.

B: IMPACT?! What do you mean, impact? Look, my wife paid for me to do something called a bungee jump, not commit hara-kiri. I mean, why on earth would I jump off there?

A: Because it gives you a buzz...

B: Look, if I wanted a buzz I'd have bought a doorbell. I think there's been a dreadful mistake.

A: Look, just try it sir... it's an amazing feeling.

B: So is having my wife nibble my earlobes, but it's not worth dying for.

A: Look, I've told you sir... you're perfectly safe. The bands pull you back up and you just dangle for a while – feeling rather exhilarated, I may add. You get a serious rush of blood to the head.

B: Not to mention a serious rush of internal organs to the head as well! I mean, you place a lot of trust in two elastic bands.

A: Sir, they're not elastic, they're rubber.

B: They are, I'm not. Cheerio. *(He goes to walk off-stage.)*

A: Sir, I've done this jump almost two hundred times and I look OK don't I?

B: *(eyes man suspiciously)* Two hundred times, eh? *(He thinks deeply.)* Hmmm. *(He goes and peers over the edge.)* Oh my...

A: Sir, the higher the better.

B: Look, listen here Monsieur Eiffel, why should I trust you, eh? Eh? How do I know you're not a loony who gets his kicks out of seeing innocent people jump to a perilous death?

A: Sir, thousands of people have done this jump. This is my job. Some people do it backwards, some do it in pairs. Some even do it naked!

B: So, you're a pervert as well as a lunatic! That doesn't help me. Look, if you want to know the truth, I'm terrified.

Pause.

A: Sir? Are you afraid of death?

B: Oh, that's encouraging. That's great, that's great! The bungee jump man is talking about death. Look, it's not death I'm afraid of, it's the ground! If I hit it too hard then death becomes a major consideration, and yes, I am afraid of it. But listen. I'm thirty-five years old, married with two lovely kids, gorgeous wife, I make forty grand a year as an accountant. I have a four bedroom detached house, a BMW, a dog called Basil and a year's subscription to Trout Fishing Monthly. I'm not about to throw it all away on a 'buzz' as you call it.

A: That's all very well sir, but listen. If you don't jump, you'll never know. You'll spend the rest of your holiday wondering how good it *might* have been, and wishing you could be here in this position again. If you do jump, I promise you'll love it, and you'll carry the memory for the rest of your life.

B: *(looking thoughtful)* Well, I suppose so. I hate to think that I'd be missing out on something if I don't. *(He stands on the edge and looks down.)* Oh God! *(He looks up and starts talking to heaven.)* I don't know why I'm speaking to you, I'll probably see you in a minute or so. *(He's very nervous and looks to the bungee man.)* Just jump, eh?

A: Sir, it's the buzz of a lifetime.

B: OK, here goes. The flight of the bumblebee. Aaaarggghhh!

He jumps (off the front of the stage if possible) with a scream of terror, which soon turns into a shout of joy, fading if possible. He has obviously loved the jump. The bungee man walks to the front of the stage and looks over.

A: See. I told you sir... great fun, eh? *(He leans forward to listen to the jumper and repeats his words.)* I'm sorry? You're coming up again for another go? OK sir, that's fine. *(He listens again.)* What do you mean you want to do it naked...?

---

1 What actions in everyday life require faith (eg flying)?

2 What persuades you to do them or not do them?

3 Why do you need faith to be a Christian?

Hebrews 11 (Living by faith)

Ephesians 3:14–19 (The security of faith in Christ)

LEADING THE BLIND

Edmund Farrow

THEME: What is a Christian?/ What do other people think of Christians?

HANDY TIPS:

Props: *a large screen or a blindfold; boards reading 'APPLAUSE' and 'OOOH'; a gag; four chairs.*

 4-5 minutes

CHARACTERS:

Cilla:
A lorra, lorra laffs. Know wha' I mean, chuck? She is fond of the odd innuendo (to say the least) and does her best to talk up the virtues of the three lovely, lovely ladies.

Roger:
A man who is just out of his depth. All the innuendo flies straight by him and he is less than impressed by the responses that the other contestants give him.

Miss Joyful (Christian 1):
She may claim to be joyful but she looks and sounds like she's been practising feeling depressed in front of a mirror.

Miss Hellfire (Christian 2):
Her church would burn heretics if it wasn't for the fact that it would make the building comfortably warm.

Miss Confused (Christian 3):
Well, let's face it, she's confused. Her Christianity is little more than inherited trappings, but that's OK. Isn't it?

Graham:
The enthusiastic voice-over man. If necessary, this part can be performed by the technician.

Technician: The technician runs around manically and looks hassled.

The sketch opens with the four contestants sitting in a row. There should be a screen between Roger and the female contestants or Roger should be wearing a blindfold. Cilla stands beside Roger, doing her hair. Miss Joyful is looking very bored and fiddling with things, Miss Hellfire is looking up some good Bible passages and Miss Confused is not quite sure where she is. The technician rushes on.

Technician: We're back on air any second now. *(He holds up three fingers, then two, then one and then a board reading 'APPLAUSE'. Cilla smiles. Either the audience applauds or the technician slaps his head in disgust. The technician rushes off.)*

Cilla: Welcome back to the show. It's getting really exciting. Will Roger here, God bless him, find true love and the woman of his dreams from among the three lovely, lovely ladies we have lined up tonight, or will he be sharing a lonely pew with his mother at church again on Sunday? How are y'feeling, chuck?

Roger: *(earnestly)* Great Cilla. I'm just so looking forward to showing one of these women what a *real* man is like.

Technician holds up a board reading 'OOOH!'

Cilla: Well, there's hope for you yet.

Roger: I don't think you've got the idea.

Cilla: Don't worry, chuck, you can show her what you really meant. *(Cilla encourages some reaction from the audience – 'Wooooo'.)* Now you've got one question left. You can ask it to all the ladies. Now what's it gonna be?

Roger: It's so tricky to decide.

Cilla: You can do it.

Roger: OK, OK! Number One, what is a Christian?

Joyful: *(sounding very depressed)* It's all about being joyful. I just have so much joy since I became a Christian, and I just want to share it with everyone. You know, I find it just so great talking to you Roger, I think we could have a great time together playing 'Scrabble'.

Cilla: What d'you think, Roger? You could be in there with some late night 'Scrabble'.

Roger: I don't know. How about you, Number Two?

Hellfire: I really have only one thing to say about being a Christian – repent now or burn forever! Give up all your wicked ways and kneel before the Lord in sackcloth and ashes, that you might be spared the judgement. Rely not on your own righteousness, but on that of the Lamb. It says in the book of Zechariah that a day will come when… *(As this goes on Cilla keeps trying unsuccessfully to break in and finally the technician rushes on with a gag and shuts Hellfire up.)*

Cilla: Right, how about it, Roger? I've heard some amazing things about sackcloth, and who knows what could happen in front of that roaring fire as you wait for those ashes?

Roger: I'm just not sure. What do you think, Number Three?

Confused: Oh, I'm a Christian. It's all about lurve. (*The technician holds up the 'OOOH' board.*) I mean love. You know, 'love your neighbour', and, er... stuff. I go to church you know... at Christmas and Easter and well, you know. I don't really understand Easter though. But my mum and dad are Christians and so that's alright then, and I'm one too. And then there's, er... Where am I?

Cilla: (*lost for words*) OK, Roger, well there you have... there you have Contestant Number Three and isn't she lovely?

Roger: (*starting to panic*) Oh, yes, they're all so, so, so...

Cilla: Don't worry, chuck. Our Graham's going to give us a summing up to help you decide.

Graham: (*over a microphone and completely hamming it up*) Thank you, Cilla. Tonight, Roger, you have a startling variety of committed women to choose from. Will you choose the really interesting Contestant Number One who enjoys working hard and playing 'Scrabble', and who regards her teddy bear as her second-best friend? Or how about the lovely Contestant Number Two, who is sure to improve your knowledge of scripture and make you feel very hot under the collar? (*'OOOH!'*). Her favourite pastime is going out in the street, yelling at people and frightening small children. And finally, there's Contestant Number Three, who devotes much of her time to collecting money for charity and whose ideal holiday is a skiing trip to Saudi Arabia.

Roger: Oh my, is that the time? (*He makes a break for it.*)

Graham: The choice is yours!

The technician runs across the stage with the 'APPLAUSE' card and the characters on stage freeze. After a pause the technician draws a finger across his throat to signal the end, and the cast walk off.

---

1 What is a Christian?
2 Can you see anything in your life, or at your church, which you think would put people off becoming a Christian?
3 How can you demonstrate Jesus Christ more attractively in your life and also in your church?

John 17:3 (Christianity = relationship with God)

I Peter 3:15,16 (Witness with gentleness and respect)

Galatians 5:16–26 (The fruits of the Spirit)

THE LAST ROLO

Matt Sands

THEME: Love / Human relationships / God's love / The gospel

HANDY TIPS:

Props: *a packet of Rolos.*

 4–5 minutes

CHARACTERS:

Narrator: the narrator is like an invisible onlooker taking the audience through the story. (S)he needs to be very animated to deal with the script. A fun character.

Wally: nervous. Loved by the audience.

Sharon: a glamour puss. A hard and confident heart-breaker.

Jesus: caring, confident and totally loveable of course.

Wally is sitting nervously on a chair, centre stage. He is obviously waiting for someone. The narrator looks at Wally and addresses the audience.

Narrator: Love. Dictionary definition: 'an intense feeling of deep affection or fondness for a person or a thing'.

He looks at Wally and presents him to the audience.

Wally – 'a foolish or inept person. In this case, also his name – the shortened form of Walter'.

Walter pulls a Rolo from his pocket, the last in an unravelled pack. He holds it up so it dangles in mid-air. He studies it carefully.

The last Rolo – 'round caramel-centred chocolate confectionery with special romantic significance. To be given to one's true love'.

55

The narrator moves behind a nervous Walter and speaks fast and loudly in his ear.

NERVOUS, CONFUSED, NAUSEATED, TERRIFIED, TRAUMATISED? *(Pause.)* See previous definition of love.

The narrator moves away from Wally, who is biting his nails and looking scared.

Object – 'a material thing that can be seen or touched'.

Desire – 'an unsatisfied longing or craving'.

Object of desire? SHARON!

On walks Sharon, posing seductively to cheers and wild applause.

Sharon – 'a babe'!

(Walter looks over and sees Sharon. He shuts his eyes and trembles even more. The narrator sees his state of fear.)

Sight – 'the faculty of seeing with the eyes'.

Wally shakes and looks terrified.

Terror – 'extreeeeeeeeme fear'.

As Sharon walks by, Wally jumps up and stands in front of her. The narrator is both impressed and surprised.

Bold – 'confidently assertive, adventurous, courageous'.

(Aside to audience.) Sucker – 'a gullible or easily deceived person'.

Walter pulls out his last Rolo and offers it to Sharon.

The last Rolo – 'round caramel-centred chocolate confectionery with special romantic significance, to be given to one's true love'.

Sharon looks and thinks. Leave a long pause here to build tension.

Time – 'the indefinite continued progress of existence, events, etc in past, present and future, regarded as a whole. Also known as the clock of the heart'.

Slap – *(Sharon slaps Wally hard in the face.)* 'A blow with the palm of the hand'.

Wally looks devastated, Sharon grabs the Rolo and drops it to the floor.

Foot – 'the lower extremity of the leg, below the ankle'.

She stamps on the Rolo and squishes it into the floor.

The last Rolo – 'squashed caramel-centred chocolate confectionery, embedded into the ground'.

Wally looks awful and stares at the Rolo as Sharon walks away triumphantly.

Aah – 'a cry of sympathy'.

He leads audience in an 'Aah' for Wally, who drops to his knees in despair. Long pause.

Broken.

Another pause, then on walks Jesus. The narrator gets excited.

Jesus – 'Son of God'.

Wally – 'the foolish or inept person'.

Jesus walks over to Wally and considers him.

Help – 'to provide what is needed or what is sought'.

Jesus picks up Wally and brushes him down. Jesus touches his own heart and then places his hand on Wally's, as a symbol of him giving Wally a new heart.

Heart – 'regarded as the centre of thought, feeling and emotion'.

New – 'of recent origin or arrival, in original condition, not worn or used'.

Jesus pulls out a last Rolo, just like Wally's.

The last Rolo – 'round caramel-centred chocolate confectionery with special romantic significance, to be given to one's true love'.

Wally smiles and takes the Rolo.

Smile – 'the facial expression of happiness'.

They embrace and begin to walk off.

Companion – 'a person who accompanies, associates with and *shares* with another'.

They exit. The narrator turns to the audience.

Love – 'an intense feeling of deep affection or fondness for a person or a thing'.

---

1   How important to you is finding a partner?

2   What are you looking for in a relationship? Why?

3   Do you put as much time or effort into developing your relation-ship with Jesus as you do in your other relationships (ie time spent chilling with your mates *and* chilling with God)?

1 John 4:17,18 (Real love)

THE MIRACLE MAN

Edmund Farrow

THEME: Evangelistic / What's life all about?/ Dealing with doubts

HANDY TIPS:

Props: *two chairs; a sheet; a garish coat; a small bottle containing brightly coloured sweets.*

   around 7 minutes

CHARACTERS:

Margie: A tired old woman who has seen it all. She is cynical and really just wants to be left alone to die. Deep down, she yearns to know why life seems so empty and unfair.

The Miracle Man:

A sarcastic magician who travels from place to place 'making dreams come true'. Unfortunately, he gives people what they *want*, rather than what they *need* and their dreams turn into nightmares. Although impatient, he is not intentionally malicious – the best he can do just isn't very good.

George and Sheila:

The ultimate middle-aged, middle-class couple. They are very polite but Sheila doesn't half go on. George is under the thumb and keeps quiet unless prompted.

Star: A teenager stuck in a really happening town – not! She spends her time dreaming about a more exciting life and is all too eager to accept a way of escaping her mundane existence.

Jason: While being a drugdealer, Jason is slimy and evil. He treats Star with contempt. As Helen's fiancé, he is initially charming but then becomes aggressive. All in all, not a pleasant man.

Helen: A normal young woman, hoping to find love.

Pat: A homeless paralytic. As written, the part is female but it could be played equally well as a male.

58

Jesus: He is concerned for Margie and is desperate for her to talk to him. He is, in turn, gentle and sharp with her, coaxing her to speak and to think. He keeps a low profile for most of the sketch, watching intently but not commenting until the end.

The stage is set with two chairs placed next to each other between centre stage and stage right. Margie sits on one of the chairs, her head in her hands. Jesus enters quietly from stage left. The others are at the rear of the stage with their backs to the audience. Pat sits, hunched over, in the middle of the line, and the rest stand. They turn to face the audience when they are needed.

Jesus: *(concerned)* Margie?

Margie: Huh? Oh, it's you again. Let me be.

Jesus: Margie, what's wrong?

Margie: I said, let me be.

Jesus: I can't – you know that. Tell me what's wrong.

Margie: It's hopeless, that's what. It's all so hopeless.

Jesus: It's not hopeless – you just have to be sure of what you hope for.

Margie: I don't understand.

Jesus: Talk to me and perhaps I can explain.

Margie: Explain? I don't want explanations and excuses. It's past that. Oh, never mind. I'm too old and I'm too tired – just let me be.

Jesus: Talk to me, Margie. Tell me what's on your mind. Tell me how you feel, tell me a story – anything. Just talk to me.

Margie: You want a story? Ha – there's only ever been one story.

Jesus: Then tell it. Let me hear what you have to say.

Margie: Oh, all right. *(She moves to the front of the stage towards stage left and speaks to the audience. Jesus moves to the side of the stage. The Miracle Man pulls on a garish coat.)* My story is about a magician. *(The Miracle Man turns to face the audience.)* He was the Miracle Man, wandering from place to place, and everywhere he went, he made dreams come true. *(Sheila and George take up positions on the chairs and mime a conversation with the Miracle Man.)* One day he was invited to the home of a middle-aged couple, who told him about their life over a polite cup of tea and a slice of fruit cake. Though they had no children, they had worked hard to keep themselves in the manner to which they had become accustomed.

Sheila: Yes, it is a nice house, isn't it? You should have seen it when we moved in though, and it's murder to heat in the winter. Isn't it dear?

George: Yes, dear.

Sheila: The bills just keep pouring in and

my husband is retiring soon. It's not like the neighbourhood is like it used to be, either. There are all sorts of people moving in and I'm afraid to go out at night.

Miracle Man: Yes, yes, this is all very well, but what do you want?

George: What do we want?

Miracle Man: Yes… Come on, come on, I don't have all day. I've got people to see, miracles to perform. What do you want?

George and Sheila confer.

George: We want security.

Miracle Man: Right. (*He walks away.*)

Margie: The Miracle Man left them, preferring to work his magic quietly, rather than employ the flashy techniques of some of his more vulgar colleagues. Time passed and the couple forgot about him as they carefully invested their money, installed burglar alarms in their house and picked friends whom they knew would not make a fuss. Their world closed in around them (*George and Sheila huddle together and hide their faces*), safe and secure, sucking the life from them. And when they died, though they had everything, they had nothing left to lose… (*Helen throws a sheet over them.*) The Miracle Man moved on until he came to a river with a young woman sitting on the bank, staring into the water. (*Star sits down at the front of the stage towards stage left and the Miracle Man walks over to her.*)

Miracle Man: What's your name?

Star: Star.

Miracle Man: (*taking the mick*) Call me Miracle. What are you looking for?

Star: Excitement.

Miracle Man: What do you want? You can expand a little this time if you like.

Star: What do I want? I want to ride on the wind. I want to reach up and grab the moon. I want to marry Brad Pitt. And I want to have fun…

Miracle Man: In this town? Who do you think I am? Paul Daniels? Oh, I'll see what I can do.

Margie: And so the Miracle Man left again and Star thought nothing more about him. But, the next day, another man came to visit her beside the river. (*Jason stalks over to Star.*)

Jason: (*evilly*) Hi there, beautiful. You're looking bored. Want some excitement?

Star: What do you know about excitement?

Jason: More than you, by the looks of it. Do you know the colour of sound? Or the sound of colour? Have you seen places that no one else has ever seen? And have you felt so good that the grass has burst into flower around your feet?

Star: No, but I want to. Tell me how. Please!

Jason: Excitement is an expensive thing. You have to buy it by the gram. But, seeing as you're a first-time customer, here's a free sample. (*He hands her a medicine bottle full of sweets.*) If you want some more, you know who to find. (*He moves off to the edge of the stage.*)

Margie: Star took the pills and then more... *(Star eats the sweets)* and more... She saw things that she could only dream about and, in so doing, turned blind to everything but herself. *(Star covers her eyes and freezes.)* The Miracle Man moved on... *(Helen stands near the front of the stage, on the opposite side from Star.)* He found another young woman standing by a bus stop and he asked his question.

Miracle Man: What do you want?

Helen: I want to be loved.

Miracle Man: Don't we all? I'll see what I can do.

Margie: The magician left and, minutes later, the woman met a young man. *(Jason strides over. Helen and Jason laugh and dance and then Jason gets down on one knee.)* There was a whirlwind romance. They laughed and danced and they were married within a month.

Helen: Yes.

Margie: Everything went wonderfully and they were happy together. Then the man became obsessive *(Jason and Helen embrace passionately but Jason won't let go)* and jealous and mean. *(Helen tries to break free but doesn't manage it completely.)*

Helen: This isn't what I wanted.

Miracle Man: Beggars can't be choosers.

Helen: But it isn't fair.

Miracle Man: Who said life was fair? What do you want? Miracles? *(Helen and Jason freeze.)*

Margie: And then the man moved on, having made all their dreams come true. And that's the end of the story. *(Depressed pause.)*

Jesus: *(moving towards Pat)* You've forgotten one.

Margie: The cripple? *(Pat uses her hands to drag herself painfully around to face the audience.)* What difference does it make?

Jesus: Hope shines brightest in the darkest place. Finish the story.

Margie: If I must. *(She clears her throat.)* Finally, the Miracle Man arrived at a dirty railway station. A penniless wretch sat there, desperate for any help that passers-by would give her.

Miracle Man: What do you want?

Pat: I want to walk.

Miracle Man: *(searching his pockets)* Well, sorry, I'm all out of miracles. Better luck next time. If you'd been a bit earlier, I...

He stops as Jesus walks over to Pat, holds out his hand and helps her to her feet so that she stands normally. Everyone stares at her and there is a hushed silence. Jesus leads her a few steps forward.

Jesus: 'The Spirit of the Lord is on me, because he has anointed me to preach good news to the poor. He has sent me to proclaim freedom for the prisoners *(he pulls away the sheet)* and recovery of sight for the blind *(he removes Star's hands from her eyes)*, to release the oppressed *(he releases Jason's grip)*, to proclaim the year of the Lord's favour.' *(pause)* Do you understand now, Margie?

Margie: Yes… No… I don't know. It's not enough. I have so many questions.

Jesus: Well then, there's hope yet. Keep talking and I'll see what I can do.

He takes her hand. They freeze.

1 Is it wrong to question God and religion?

2 What are your plans for your life? Do you think that God has any plans for your life? Are yours and his the same?

3 How do we deal with the fact that there's suffering and that not everything around us is good?

Luke 4:18,19 (Jesus' mission statement: 'The Spirit of the Lord is on me …')

Jeremiah 29 (Trusting in God's plans for our lives)

Psalm 73 (Trusting God through questions/doubts/suffering)